LIFE, DEATH, GRIEF, AND THE POSSIBILITY OF PLEASURE

By Oceana Sawyer

Life, Death, Grief, and the Possibility of Pleasure
Published through Good to Better Group

All rights reserved
Copyright © 2022 by Oceana Sawyer
Cover art copyright © 2022 by Oscar Keys

Excerpted and reprinted by permission from Micheala Hass, *The Sounds of Healing* for "Reasons to be Cheerful" website, July 16, 2021.

ISBN: 978-0-57-837247-1 (Paperback Edition)
ISBN: 978-0-57-837248-8 (eBook Edition)

No part of this publication may be reproduced, stored in a retrieval system, or transmitted in any form or by any means electronic, mechanical, photocopying, recording, or otherwise, without the written permission of the author or publisher.

Dedication

To my mother, Vivian Wilcox Lott, who loved me thoroughly enough to always tell me the truth. Though she often disagreed with my choices, she remained proud of me regardless.

From the moment I published my first short story, "The Quay," at the age of twelve, she has been waiting for my first book. Sadly, she did not live to see it. Nonetheless, it is dedicated to her because she willed it into being with her ceaseless devotion and belief.

I will love you forever, Mom.

Table of Contents

Acknowledgements vii

Prologue ix

Introduction xiii

Chapter 1 The Case for Pleasure 1

Chapter 2 The Art of Creating Evermore Pleasure 11

Chapter 3 Cultivating a More Pleasurable Lifestyle 21

Chapter 4 My Story 35

Chapter 5 Pleasure Applied to Dying and Grieving 45

Chapter 6 Bringing It All Together 65

Epilogue 83

Acknowledgements

First and foremost, I want to acknowledge my editor, Leslie Quigless. This book would never have come into being without her. I know everyone says that about their editor, but I'm serious. I dropped this project so many times only to have her poke me for the next chapter. In the most gentle and deft manner, she never gave my self-doubt an ounce of reality. Her skill informed me, and our interplay was magical such that the best of my capacity emerged. She was true to her word in that this is, indeed, in our humble opinion, a jewel box of a book: small but beautifully written.

Next, I must give a shout-out to the amazing people who readily and enthusiastically contributed supplemental content. I had a very short list of people whose work I admired and that aligned with the themes of this book. These, in particular, are also people I know personally and adore. Melanie, Naila, Ash, Roshni, you are indeed kin.

Velda Thomas, Lisbeth White, and Anne Marie Keppel got me across the finish line with their considered advice and endless support born out of direct experience.

Of the many teachers and mentors whose shoulders I stand upon and to whom I could never express the depth of my gratitude, I must first and foremost acknowledge, Vic Baranco. He advocated for my pleasure, particularly as a Black woman, long before I could do it for myself. Also, I am enormously grateful to Cindy Baranco, Jackie Van Sinderen, Suzie Baranco, Marilyn Moohr, Francesca Arnoldy, Alua Arthur, Lashanna Williams, and not the least of which, Resmaa Menakem.

I must, of course, offer a deep bow to the love of my life, George Sawyer. His unwavering love and devotion have made it possible for me to explore to my heart's content all the finest things, and with whom I've had the greatest adventures of a lifetime, including this one.

Finally, I give heartfelt appreciation to all the friends and colleagues who inspired and/or informed the thinking contained herein through many hours of conversation, laughter, and deep sighs, including Millie Gross, Michelle Phillips, Donna Baker, Naomi Edmondson, Colin Selig, Mary Ann Shekeloff and every single one of my patrons on Patreon. You have all been the wind beneath my wings these past two years.

Prologue

In 2020, I got this idea for a little book. Something spare but packed with sweetness and inspiration for some other ways of living, dying, and grieving. Some hope filled ways that could be added on to the myriad of well-researched methodologies that already existed. You know, those ways that you stumble upon because you've tried everything else and they've been useful, but you still have a small bit of desire for something more. This little book is an offer to that desire.

When I discovered a couple years ago that my mother, whom I loved dearly, was going to die within a few months, I felt profound grief (more specifically known as anticipatory grief). Through the lens of my work as a death doula, however, and within the context of a supportive community and my unique sensual perspective, I experienced genuine curiosity about my grief process. I knew that her dying, and her subsequent death, could be a profound spiritual opening—if I were willing to surrender to the big, complicated emotions that encompassed my grief: sadness, fear, anger, and even love. And I knew that the degree of surrender I sought would be most possible via my own physicality; or rather, via my own capacity to feel and process with my senses: in other words, my own sensuality.

It was natural, then, for me to find information about and expression of my grief through my body. Swimming, sensual pleasure, walks in nature, culinary adventures, acupuncture, bodywork, and music were all sources of healing. I also worked with an online grief therapist for the periods I felt ready to go deeper.

The confluence of all these factors—my commitment to consciously opening to all of my experience; my sensual approach to the process; the support from my community and partner; and a bit of therapy—enabled me to experience my grief as a spacious, natural, and raw entity that wanted, in the most genuine and purest sense, to be felt.

And I did feel it. As a result, I perceived a sense of sweetness almost, a benevolence, I had not before known. In the midst and at the bottom of even my pulpiest moments, it surrounded me like a warm blanket. I couldn't help but come from that place with the people with whom I interacted. The first few weeks of my mother's death were a whirlwind of activity; yet I experienced them in slow motion, a kind of time out of time, that allowed me to slow down enough to truly be with my loved ones and my own experience.

Then the coronavirus exploded onto the scene, quickly followed by the ignition of a racial awakening/reckoning. Both of these physically impactful and horrific circumstances further expanded and deepened the experience of grief in my world. Meditation and gentle forms of yoga soothed me, as well as books, podcasts, and body-centered workshops.

Though the onslaught of emotion brought on by the twin tidal waves of COVID-19 and the violence against Black bodies was, at times, as overwhelming for me as it was for so many, I felt largely anchored. Even in the aftermath of my mother's death, I could feel this anchoring. Big emotions—outrage and helplessness and terror—swept through me, yes. But I was present to them. I was with them with all of my body, all of my being. So, much of the time, instead of feeling drowned by my tears and internal (and external) screams, I was able to ride them. Surf them.

This sensation of being with difficult emotions, I came to realize, truly is the body at its holiest. At its realest. At its truest. And, thus, at its most pleasured. For pleasure as I'm defining it doesn't exclude pain. Rather, true pleasure is the conscious, felt integration of every emotion through the body, and those emotions very much include the large, difficult, and most painful ones—the ones we most want to push away.

And here's the beauty of that integration: the more pain you are able to truly, consciously feel and integrate through the body, the more pleasure, the more awe, the more glory you are able to truly, consciously feel and integrate through the body as well.

My experiences with death and grief have led me to a rather stunning conclusion: that body-centered death care encompassing pleasure can increase one's capacity for personal expansion. It's an idea that has redefined my work as an end-of-life doula.

The notions of the body, the senses, death, grief, and pleasure don't go together in our society. We isolate them from each other. However, I believe we do so to our detriment. I also believe, though, that if we take a more holistic, open, and less fearful approach to death; and if we are bold enough to reimagine what the death experience, and what grief and outrage and even fear can look like, then we have the capacity to truly expand our human potential for spiritual evolution. And we can do so right here, right now, in our very own humble—and very holy—bodies.

Introduction

Reading non-fiction in an orderly manner is a habit of mine. Sometimes I do. Often, I don't. I recommend that you consume this book in whatever way pleases you. That which pleases you is the point of this entire endeavor. However, I will say that the chapters do build upon themselves in the way that they are presented.

While there are references to death and grief throughout, the first four of the six chapters focus on establishing a pleasure perspective in ordinary life. There are two reasons for this. First, I hold the point of view that energy can never be destroyed. Similarly, like people from many indigenous cultures, I believe that from the moment you are conceived you are physically living until your body ceases to function. In that context, cultivating pleasure in life includes the dying process.

Second, tending to your whole life is the best foundation for being able to access pleasure, if you choose, regardless of what is happening—whether it's giving birth, actively dying, grieving, or any other of the myriad of activities that comprise a lifetime.

It's also important to note that this book contains minuscule amounts of medical, psychological, or religious information. I claim no medical education or training aside from certified nursing assistant training, which is more than three decades old. Also, while I have psychological education and training, I am not, nor have I ever been, licensed. Moreover, there are already dozens of excellent books in the end-of-life sphere that cover specific topics on dying and grieving in great detail.

What I do have is education, training, experience, and more importantly passion in the realm of sensuality, spirituality, liberation, and a particular aspect of end-of-life care. It is from that narrow perspective that I put forth some ideas and practices that are intended to add to, rather than replace, ideas and methodologies that the reader is already using in their journey with dying and grieving. Everything contained in these pages is that which I have lived and found valuable.

Additionally, I wish to state that in so far as everyone dies, there are too many who die violently, accidentally, suddenly, or by negligence through no wish of their own. Those deaths are tragic and are to be acknowledged and honored. They are not included in the purview of this book. Perhaps that will be a book for another time, as I do feel it to be an important and relevant topic for consideration.

It is also worth noting that I do not have any trauma-informed training, and there may be aspects of this book that will run counter to that substantial body of information. If you are in the midst of working through loss from that perspective, the proceeding content may not be useful, and possibly even activating, for you. The same is true for anyone diagnosed and experiencing complicated grief.

I'm sure there are more caveats that ought to be given, but here I will say that generally speaking, die and grieve any way you want. There is no "wrong" way to do either. However you are doing it, IS the right way. What is on offer here are some additional options to consider. None of these options will be new. You may have already considered them, or perhaps you are employing them even now. If that is the case, then I hope you find validation and a cheerleader herein.

In any case, I encourage an open mind and heart if you decide to proceed with the journey of consuming the forthcoming content. May you find joy and recognition.

Chapter 1

The Case for Pleasure

The Missing Element

When we talk about caring for ourselves and loved ones over the course of our lives, we might speak of exercising, eating nutrient-dense foods, and getting enough sleep. When we talk about caring for ourselves and loved ones as the time of death draws nigh, we might speak of pain management, comfort care, and breathing. While all of these elements certainly are significant to our living and dying well, I believe one critical component has been overlooked in both seasons of life: pleasure.

If your eyebrows rose in some surprise, you're not alone. Culturally, we don't value pleasure, which I'll define here as simply feeling good. I contend, though, that pleasure is a vital aspect of our wellbeing and humanity, and that consciously considering it as we live, die, and grieve will improve our experiences immeasurably.

This is such a big and lovely idea that I want to explore it in some depth. Let's start with a rather audacious hypothesis that pleasure is not only important to us but also the point of it all!

Why Pleasure Is the Point!

Every decision, every move you make in a given moment, is the best-feeling thing you can think to do at that time. The sheer fact that you're doing it means it's the thing you think will make you feel the most good. No sane person sits around thinking, *What is the worst thing I can do or say right now?* Even if you're having that precise thought, your goal is, at bottom, a means toward feeling good.

The point isn't to judge your goals; rather, it's to show that we are always reaching for what feels good to us in a given moment—whether or not we are conscious of that intention.

So why not be deliberate about it? When you deliberately seek the most pleasurable option in a given situation, you generate a higher and more satisfying quality of pleasure than you would if you didn't proceed in this fashion. This is because the goal of creating and consuming pleasure leads to nothing less than higher standards of experience and expanded consciousness. Sounds lofty, I know, but consider this idea:

> *If you have the goal of making an experience more pleasurable—and this idea applies to just about any experience, including dying and grieving—that goal is necessarily going to lead to a higher quality of experience. And if you are consistent, your standards as a whole will rise over time and uplift your overall quality of life.*

For example, I am at my desk typing these words with a specific time frame to accomplish the task. Now, I could just pound out the words. Instead, I've prepared my favorite tea, lit a rose-scented candle, and turned on my Soul Fulfilling playlist on Spotify. By taking these steps, I've elevated my writing experience to a sensually pleasing one that is expanding not only the present moment act of writing but also the *actual ideas* that are emerging within this pleasurable context. I decided to make the experience of writing more pleasurable, and as a result, my basic needs are met, yes; but because I also feel good performing the task, the work itself is likely better than what it would be otherwise.

Practicing Pleasure in a Pleasure-resistant Culture

It makes sense that you might be resistant to creating more pleasure for yourself. Mainstream American culture is rooted in white supremacist Puritanism. This belief system put a premium on personal sacrifice and maniacal hard work and punished most anything that felt good. Accordingly, this system made villains of the Indigenous folk, who understood how to live in balance with the entirety of the ecosystem wherever they were located—and thus, did so with great pleasure.

Even worldwide, though, all three major religions (Islam, Judaism, and Christianity) preach pain and sacrifice as a way—sometimes, the only way—to gain access to heavenly rewards. In this context, viewing pleasure as a healthy, healing force would necessarily be suspect.

Thus, we have largely been conditioned to be suspicious of pleasure; therefore, we do not value it. We instead trust in and value hard work, sacrifice, and suffering as a moral high road and a means to earn whatever good can be gleaned in life. In addition, many of us learn quickly that comfort and pleasure is not part of our birthright for a variety of reasons having to do with not being a cisgendered male of European descent. As a result, we lead lives that are dominated by discomfort and good—but not great and beyond—experiences.

The Path of Pleasure Isn't Easy

Interestingly enough, the path of pleasure is paved with…well, pleasure. Learning how to feel better and better is evermore restorative—and fun—on every level! So that as you're engaged in the process of creating your life, the solutions that arise feel better and more authentic. You move through the world and your day with greater ease, generosity, and spaciousness. More starts going your way, and you have the experience of the wind at your back.

I'll make zero bones about it: pursuing a path of pleasure can, and most likely *will*, make you a target of derision. That part is real. It is very likely that your friends and family could regard you as lacking in drive and self-control if you begin making choices that involve fun, pleasure, and/or comfort. Their concern, fear, or even contempt for your changes reflects the cultural expectation that we will sacrifice our comfort for subscription to the mainstream "no pain, no gain" philosophy.

There are three ways to deal with that energy coming towards you. You can change your behavior to be more consistent with societal expectations. You could also just keep doing what you're doing and ignore the responses. Third, you could engage your detractors in dialogue about why you're doing what you're doing. You could even look for creative ways to engage them if your initial efforts fall short.

I recently posted some interesting facts about myself on social media, including that I enjoy laughing, sometimes even in sad or scary situations. It can be a way for me to mindfully decrease tension and increase my comfort. Someone responded that he would not want that characteristic in his death doula. To that, I replied, "You should have exactly the doula that suits you." (And yes, I was chuckling as I replied.)

So, while the path of pleasure yields enormous rewards, it also requires equanimity in the face of others' reactions, along with some humor and self-compassion for the missteps you're sure to take along the way. Additionally, the path requires your *attention*, as you must continually listen within to see how you're feeling and adjust accordingly.

Next, we'll explore the simple, step-by-step process that will hone your attention skills and help you begin creating more pleasure in your life. In the meantime, look for ways you can make one task more pleasurable today.

Risa is a good example of someone who spent several years cultivating a pleasurable lifestyle, who was able to rely upon it at the end of their days.

⁂ Risa ⁂

In January 2021, I wrote this question to my client, Risa: *"I would love to find out from your perspective what role pleasure is playing in this last phase of your life."* The following is her response.

Having a calm, happy relationship with death and putting end-of-life details in place that please me has made me happy and lightened my load and Yon's load. And it may also be beginning to lighten the loads of my close friends and family. Sometimes we make terrible jokes about it.

It also seems to have given me more freedom to be both kinder and more forthright in my communication with others. I don't hold back as much, and at the same time, how I communicate is taking on a level of skill in being kind that I didn't know I could exercise. I recall Victor telling me that if I were really Yon's friend, I wouldn't let him be an asshole. To be effective in stopping asshole behavior in those we love (and in myself), I have to be kind, straightforward, and truthful. I may do it better now.

Also, it helps me to talk about stuff with Yon and see clearly what I can put in place and what is really not for me to do or decide at all. It belongs to the living. It's great to not overly control every little detail. My therapist reminded me of something Victor said about making one's desires known and letting others execute them their own way. She said, people who are grieving go through their own process and especially Yon will need practical, linear stuff to help him go through his. I'm not doing him a favor by trying to take too much out of his hands. He agrees with this point of view.

- ꙮ It's been fun asking specific family and friends to help do specific things. The perfect hats for my tender chemo scalp came from long-time friends.
- ꙮ Rachel to lay a medicine wheel on my grave.
- ꙮ My sister to come down and just be with us when the time is close, hopefully well after the worst of COVID-19 has passed. And also, to be the succeeding trustee for our living trust to support the surviving spouse and complete distribution when we are both gone.

LIFE, DEATH, GRIEF, AND THE POSSIBILITY OF PLEASURE

- ꙮ Keiko and Toni to distribute my medicine objects as listed.
- ꙮ Asking my immediate family if there is something of mine they would like.
- ꙮ Toni wisely said, do not put their names on your belongings while you are alive, as they are still yours. Take photographs, number and describe them, and make a list to be handled well after you die. Be alive while you are alive and dead when you are dead.

One joyful action this process contributed to was to give my son one of my mom's few heirloom jewelry pieces that I had, a simple but dramatic throat pit-length pendant with six diamonds to give his girlfriend on their one year anniversary since she claimed him as hers. I felt very happy doing this. Gently polishing up the diamonds in warm water and gentle dish liquid was a thrill. And passing on something at the right time. She is Filipino, so from her culture, a gift via his mother and grandmother was a big deal. It looks fabulous with her warm skin and dark features. She cried for quite a while. Then later let him take her photo wearing the necklace. It is so hers and he is so hers. I am happy to pass on something that represents my mom's best good fortune, being a master of later life true love. They traveled around the world together for a few years and then married when she was fifty and he sixty-three, and they were each other's greatest treasure for her last thirty-plus years of life. My grandmother was also a master of late life love when the love of her early life returned decades later, and they married. Her rings will go to my daughter.

Another thing that this process puts into fine focus is certainty about where I put my attention. I do not squander it on things that are fruitless, like my own or others' fussing and whining cycles. That uses energy, which I am not willing to give. This doesn't mean I don't pay attention to serious business in my loved one's lives or in the world, like the ongoing struggles for health, joy, equality, and justice, but I am careful to try to only witness or take in as much as I can process and act on with gratification, even if small. I am clearer about what is and is not my job.

The COVID-19 pandemic has actually made my life as an introvert easier. I like Zoom in small doses and using the phone, emails, and texts more when it feels good. It helps me turn inward happily. That and preparing for dying.

I enjoyed writing a few thousand postcards to disenfranchised voters in key voter suppression states and putting together a few thousand more cards in complete postcarding packets for others—many high-risk folks—so they could minimize exposure to public places and do no contact pick-up of all the supplies on my porch. I feel gratified contributing to justice, equality, and democracy in our country and directly fighting racist, sexist, ageist, and classist voter suppression through person-to-person, old-fashioned handwritten cards.

What does this have to do with the dying process? It is a meditation for me and works as physical and emotional pain management. Fighting cancer and waiting to die is boring. The choice to be in pleasure rather than boredom leads me to do what pleases me each day. It pleases me to do what is within my grasp, which both aims at a world that can be better and serves my happiness.

My writing partner and sister by declaration, Toni and I, have been having Zoom calls once or twice a week to work on our novels. It's something that gives us both a lot of pleasure.

I think understanding this phase in our and our loved ones' lives contributes to being more dedicated to making time for what and who we love.

Saturday, I Facetimed my sister, and she answered from a chairlift and took me by phone on a ski run with her and her friends. Fabulous. Then I took a nap.

My friend Joe'l joined my bouts of swimming in the bay in the late fall, early winter. When I could no longer swim due to chemo and a kidney issue, I lent her the warm dive hood from my sister, and neoprene socks to make her swim more comfy and fun and asked her to swim for me, too. Vicarious pleasure works, too.

Not sure if these thoughts and examples are in the range of your question, but in considering pleasure in my life at this time and how that's been related to making a clear relationship with the end of my life, these are some that rose to the top.

Chapter 2

The Art of Creating Evermore Pleasure

Now, let's look more deeply at the nature of pleasure and examine the simple, step-by-step process that will enable you to begin creating more pleasure in your life immediately.

Defining pleasure is a good place to start. For me, it simply means feeling good within your body and spirit in any given moment. Pleasure is manifested in the six senses: sight, sound, smell, taste, touch, and thoughts/memories. Your senses are your instruments of pleasure.

What Pleasure Requires

Just as your senses aren't static, neither is pleasure. Rather, it is a dynamic force that requires some rigor in your attention—at least at first. This is because what feels good in your body one moment may not feel good the next, and you'll need to continuously bring your attention back to how you are feeling and adjust accordingly.

For instance, dancing may start off feeling cathartic and joyful; but then arrives a moment when you realize, you're out of breath. Or perhaps your knees begin twinging.

Next, you could ask yourself, "What is the next most pleasurable thing to do from here?"

It may be that you slow your movements; change the music; or simply stand still and *feel,* allowing emotions or truth to bubble up and inform your next act. If you are willing to pay attention so that whatever would feel good next can drop in, you can continue spiraling up into ever-increasing experiences of pleasure.

Pleasure Defies Formulas

Here's the twist, though: *you cannot produce—or reproduce—pleasure in a formulaic manner.*

Whatever worked last time, may or may not work next time. Pleasure truly is a moment-to-moment proposition that asks you to return continually to the present moment and check in with yourself, with your body. With this level of attention, you'll notice that the amount of good you are experiencing is always either increasing or decreasing, however minutely. If you are willing to keep paying attention to what is feeling good, you can discover whether the next moment can feel even better with a slight change.

In this moment-to-moment manner, you can create your experience. In fact, you can create your whole life! In my experience, this is the way life can feel fresh, like an adventure. And relatively quickly, you'll notice a growing propensity for feeling good in your body for no particular reason. You'll realize pleasure as its own reward—the *only* reward, really. Because if it—whatever "it" is for you (success, money, love)—doesn't feel good in the moment… what's the point?

Pleasure and Presence

You may have noticed how words like "presence" and "attention"—words typically used to describe Eastern meditation techniques—are surfacing in our discussion of pleasure. This is because true meditation and true pleasure both place you squarely in the "now." The practice of pleasure, then, can accurately be described as a meditative one.

You could even pursue this path of pleasure much like the path of dharma: with discipline, rigor, and nonattachment. It may sound counterintuitive to apply nonattachment to pleasure. However, as stated earlier, pleasure is a moment-to-moment proposition that is best cultivated with attention to, even delight in, the present moment. The next moment may not be quite as delightful; and so, a letting go of what previously just worked will be necessary to allow for the slight or complete adjustment needed to continue feeling good.

Integrity in Pleasure

Rigor in the form of integrity is also useful. Integrity goes hand-in-hand with attention when it comes to creating pleasure; for true pleasure, actually feeling good, cannot be faked. This requires a certain amount of self-awareness and courage to be willing to tell the truth to yourself, at the minimum.

In fact, the truth can be one of the most primal forms of pleasure. Ever notice how your body feels when truth, either your own or someone else's, is being spoken? Perhaps a warm, electric shimmer of sensation courses through your being. We often call this response "goosebumps" because there may be tiny bumps on the skin as evidence. The next feeling we notice may be relief so intense, it's akin to a mini orgasm. You may, in fact, have a range of sensual bodily experiences: shortness of breath, rapid heart rate, a pleasant taste in your mouth, a change in vision, and hearing either acute or dulled. These bodily sensations may be brief but are palpable and powerful. This is because they are truth resonating, vibrating, on the densest, most pleasurable level possible—in your very own body.

Of course, there are also "hard" truths. The pleasure may not be immediate—often, quite the opposite! If we are willing to remain attentive to our bodily sensations, though, we will typically reach a point of recognition that something useful, possibly even transformative, has transpired. That moment of recognition is uplifting and can feel like a jolt of delicious energy.

For example, a fashion stylist once gave me feedback about changes I needed to make to my hair—feedback I initially took personally. My immediate response was to be critical of myself ("I've been looking ridiculous this whole time!") and then her ("She's so mean!"). However, I knew the truth of the stylist's feedback through my bodily sensations: that familiar pit in my belly; a quiet hum in my chest cavity. My body knew the stylist was right. And so, although I sulked the entire time, I made the changes. And I could feel the rightness of that decision in my body.

The end result, by the way, was gorgeous.

Ready for Some Pleasure Practice?

In order to demonstrate the practicality and flexibility of practicing pleasure, let's look at how we can bring even the reading of this chapter to a pleasurable close. Don't worry, the below steps will take only a couple minutes and will work whether you're reading on your phone, tablet, or computer! (And it's fine for you to open and close your eyes to read the steps as necessary.)

1. Close your eyes.
2. Take a deep breath; let it go.
3. Simply notice how you're feeling in your body.
4. Open your eyes and look around.
5. Using any of your six senses, find one thing that delights you in the current moment. Or find one thing you *can* find delightful.
    - It could be the sound of birds; some music; the bright green of the grass outside; a house plant; or perhaps the beverage you're sipping is pretty good; or maybe you notice the cotton of the top you're wearing is quite soft and feels yummy on your skin. You get the gist.
6. Once you have located one thing, put your complete attention on it and see if you can enjoy it even more, just with your attention and positive regard.
7. Ask yourself, "Is there one thing I could do that would make this experience feel even better?"
    - The answer may be no, which is fine. The magic is in asking the question.
    - Alternately, the answer may be to simply sit for a minute longer and put your attention on your one thing, or to relax more.
    - Alternatively, the answer may be to add in another one of your senses to complement the one that has your attention. For instance, maybe

you'd like to turn on some music or prepare a cup of tea.
- 🙏 Do that one thing. (Or decide it would be more pleasurable not to!)
8. Continue enjoying your sensory experience for another moment.
9. Close your eyes and notice how you feel.
10. When you're ready, open your eyes and continue reading the chapter.

Congratulations! You've just created a more pleasurable moment, and day, and life for yourself in mere minutes! All the pleasure you create in your world—this bit included—creates a thread in the tapestry of a life customized to suit you. And since pleasure can enhance all of life's seasons, we'll soon examine how to apply the above practice within death and grief care.

Here is another invitation to explore further offered by Roshni Kavate.

Roshni is an Artist, Healer, and Activist. Roshni Kavate is the Founder and Creative Director of Cardamom and Kavate, a wellness platform dedicated to reclaiming nourishing practices rooted in ancestral wisdom for collective liberation. She believes grief is a portal to wholeness.

❦ Roshni Kavate ❦

Grief and Comfort Food

Lemon rice is my ultimate comfort food. It has fragrant rice as a base, toasted pea-nuts for the perfect crunch, lemon for zing, curry leaves for aromatics, and tangy green mango for a surprising finish. We ate this lemon rice at festivals, on long train and bus rides to visit grandparents, or as a satisfying quick meal after coming home from a long trip with nothing but dry goods in the pantry. The peanuts are a reminder of another era for me. My childhood is filled with memories of eating freshly boiled peanuts strewn on a newspaper with my mother, grandmother, and the rest of my family. The salty broth of a fresh boiled peanut is ambrosia.

My grandmother is no longer alive, and I live across the world from my mom. But when I miss home, when I am sad, when I am celebrating, I always look back to the comfort foods of my family. Craving the comfort of food in hard times and good times is universal, as is the grief we carry within our bodies. It could be the loss of loved ones, of lives and dreams we imagined together but now gone. Of not knowing the land of our birth, of being rejected, the grief of yearning to be accepted, to be home, to be well in our bodies. Cooking and eating are primal rituals that we partake in every day, many times a day. They nourish our bodies, heal our spirit, remind us of where we come from, and connect us with our resilient ancestors.

In my experience as a palliative care nurse, I was struck by my patients' wishes at the end of their lives. They would yearn for a bright green mango with bagoong from their childhood—one they still remembered seventy years later. They would long for the warmth of a pot of beans, the lovingly wrapped onigiri with a vibrant umeboshi plum, a fragrant sweet potato pie with cinnamon to celebrate the holidays.

Grief can feel like a cloudy, numb existence where we feel we are fading from life. Yet grief is a visceral invitation to rediscover the sensuality of our being. We can offer our grieving self sweetness with a bowl of fruit, or a moment of ease with a cup of rich broth. A pot of stew can be an unspoken yet powerful reassurance for a dear friend. It is an act of deep care and a step towards re-humanizing ourselves.

Reclaiming my ancestral comfort foods has turned into an act of political practice for me. My family first suffered under British colonization and then struggled in post partition India, losing their vibrant legacy as artisans and entrepreneurs. There was a palpable darkness and gloom that I couldn't identify, but what I remember is plump little shrimp with ginger and golden onions, goat leg curries, hearty heirloom greens, and flatbreads made with grains harvested fresh that season. What I remember is turmeric, ginger, chilies, and coriander carefully sun dried and blended at the mill next door. A home-cooked meal was a reminder of joy and aliveness even in the face of despair and survival.

Each time we cook our ancestral foods, we are keeping the memories of our families alive and affirming our own vitality no matter the depth of grief within us. We are remembering the taste of ease: a ripe, juicy whole mango as an invitation to awaken the intelligence in our cellular memory. Food and cooking can offer a balm for our grief. If we can listen to it and befriend it, it can unearth the wisdom of returning to our wholeness.

I remember my dad casually slipping me chili coconut-dusted peanuts and a sip of ice cold sudsy Indian beer at age twelve as a precursor to a long mutton biryani lunch with my extended family. When I cook a lamb biryani on a Sunday, I am celebrating my longing for meals that were cooked and eaten as a large, intergenerational family; unhurried; the comforting presence of knowing you will always be fed, and always be cared for.

My grief has been craving dal, rice, ghee eaten with my hands, garlicky clams, bucatini piled high with spicy tomato sauce, bowls of okra with crispy onions.

My invitation is to ask yourself the following: What is my grief craving?

Chapter 3

Cultivating a More Pleasurable Lifestyle

We'll soon apply all we're learning about pleasure to grief and dying; but I first want to ensure you're able to create a pleasurable life not only moment-to-moment, but with a big picture perspective as well. If you have that level of perspective, you'll be able to shape your life all the way through the end of it, as well as grieve your losses in such a way that it is deliberately geared/oriented toward feeling good.

I always like to begin with my definition of pleasure. Again, it simply means feeling good within your body and spirit in any given moment. Pleasure is a sensual sensation and thus is manifested in the six senses: sight, sound, smell, taste, touch, and thoughts/memories. Your senses are your instruments of pleasure.

Now, let's look at steps you can take to cultivate a more pleasurable lifestyle.

Pleasure Mapping

Cultivating more pleasure in your life can initially seem, at best, a vague goal, and at worst, overwhelming.

Once we recall how pleasure works, however, we can simply examine what we find pleasing to our senses and invest in whatever we find.

Beginning with an inventory of what constitutes pleasure for you greatly increases the probability of your creating a lifestyle of pleasure, because when you're done, you have your very own pleasure map: those places, things, actions, and thoughts to which you can devote evermore energy and become an evermore pleasure-oriented person.

As valuable as pleasure mapping is, it takes only a few minutes. As you'll see, we can ask some concrete questions that will reveal the unique shape a pleasurable lifestyle can have. The great news is that there are as many pleasurable lifestyle shapes as there are people!

Pull out a pen and sheet of paper (or your laptop) and answer the following questions:

1) What do I enjoy visually?
2) What sounds appeal to me?
3) What are yummy tastes for me?
4) What feels good on my skin?
5) How do I like to be touched?
6) What smells delight me?
7) What thoughts ease my mind or make me laugh or smile?

Notice that you're addressing all six of your senses, including your sixth sense of thought/memory. Again, your senses are the means through which you experience pleasure.

Notice that all these pleasures are of the present moment—meaning, they can only be enacted and felt in the present moment. This is because pleasure is grounded in experiencing yourself in the here and now. Pleasure provides a tangible means of learning how to be present.

Here are a few answers from my list.

1) What do I enjoy visually?
   Natural candlelight, Rege Jean Page

2) What sounds appeal to me?
   Kora music, laughter, waves crashing

3) What are yummy tastes for me?
   Pinot noir, French fries, chai tea

4) What feels good on my skin?
   Silk, a firm hand, warm water

5) How do I like to be touched?
   With attention and intention

6) What smells delight me?
   Lily of the valley flowers, sandalwood incense, my dogs

7) What thoughts ease my mind or make me laugh or smile?
   My ancestors, my niece's smile, "Season 1, Episode 7" of Lovecraft Country

A Pleasurable Lifestyle Is a Deliberate Choice

We live in a society that is more oriented to numbness on a good day and suffering on most others. This is, in part, a result of our industrialized economic engine, which requires that we labor and produce five-plus days and forty-plus hours per week, week in and week out, regardless of how we feel. In addition, mainstream religion espouses sacrifice as a requirement to get to heaven. Structural white supremacy also contributes to the collective orientation toward pain, as it devalues any person or being that is not an able-bodied, white, cisgendered male of means. Left to our own devices, as molded by our default conditioning, then we will most likely not choose feeling as good as we can.

Creating a pleasurable lifestyle is therefore a deliberate act—even a revolutionary one. (I'd argue it's a personally evolutionary act as well!) And because, again, we're acting against our default conditioning, creating a pleasurable lifestyle is also an act we must choose over and over again. We're creating the new habit of not only feeling good but also *valuing and investing in* feeling good.

Deliberately creating a pleasurable lifestyle may initially take more effort, especially if the concepts we are discussing are new to you. You'll have to pause and think more about how you are feeling and take steps, small or big, to feel better and better. Once you commit to feeling good in principle, however, you will find you won't have to make that much more effort. Also, over time, checking in with yourself about how you're feeling will become second-nature or a way of being—something that won't take any more effort than routine actions that make life decent, like grocery shopping or making your bed.

Here are the efforts I make that result in my life being more pleasurable. Related to my previous list:

- I keep candles, incense, and wine in stock at all times.
- I create and update my Spotify playlists curated with kora music for daytime and ocean waves for sleeping when I want it.
- I regularly schedule massages.
- When I attend those massages, I communicate to massage therapists about how I like to be touched and give positive feedback often.
- I simply stop and take in whatever beauty is in my line of sight. As I type this sentence, I'm taking in the sunlight on the trees and moist green grass outside my window.

Change One Thing

Now that you have a good list, pick one item on it, and play with it. See if you can find a way for that thing to feel even better by experimenting with changing one thing.

For example, I like natural light, so I'm always playing with the curtains and the blinds in my house, or turning off artificial lights to get the lighting just right. Taking the extra time isn't a bother to me because I'm creating more pleasure for myself.

Now, it's your turn. Perhaps you like having fresh air in your bedroom. If so, how much? If having all the windows open is lovely for a few minutes before you get chilly, does it feel even better if you close the windows a little bit? What is the exact right amount for the window to be open for you to have fresh air and still be comfortable in terms of temperature? Teasing out this idea, and then trying it out, will expand your pleasure, and thus, your pleasure capacity.

What Is Pleasure Capacity?

Everyone possesses pleasure capacity, which we'll define here as *the innate capacity to feel evermore good via one's senses.* It's a natural part of our human packaging.

Our ability to cultivate our pleasure capacity, however, varies according to our individual willingness to nurture this power. It's helpful to think of it as a muscle that grows as we engage with our pleasure maps and put our attention on what feels good to us. Incredibly, pleasure capacity is a muscle we can grow all our lives.

This being said, here I want to acknowledge that many people have had traumatic experiences, the consequences of which they are living with on a daily basis. These experiences have affected the way they experience pleasure in very real ways. It doesn't mean that the capacity for feeling good is outside of their purview. It could mean that there are slow and thoughtful ways for accessing it that can be cultivated when the person is ready to do so, and not one minute before.

As I said in the introduction, this is not my area of expertise, and as such I defer to more in-depth experience and research in this area.

The Belief That Pleasure Is Bad

You may wonder why more of us don't develop our pleasure capacity if we all have the raw material—our senses—to do so.

The reason is that we tend to be suspicious of people who consciously cultivate pleasure. We think spending time on feeling good for its own sake is selfish, lazy, and demonstrates poor character. That is the programming we get from our religious and cultural institutions. People pursuing pleasure can seem weird and uncontrollable to most folks because they are behaving outside of what is considered normal by the standards of our society. To be conscious of what pleases you and willing to consume it makes you a bit of a rebel in a culture that promotes sacrifice and suffering.

Because of this, you may feel a bit isolated at times. You'll also feel liberated! Instead of blowing past or deflecting the unexpected bits of pleasure you receive as you may have before, you'll say yes more and more. And when you consume what feels good to you, you become one of the rare people in the world who is actually gratified. You become a delightful person to be around, and you inspire others to allow more good for themselves, too. When you begin paying attention to your pleasure capacity, you'll realize that pleasure cultivation is an act of lovingkindness that creates evermore good in the world.

Simply Say Yes!

Increasing your capacity for pleasure looks, first of all and most simply, like saying yes to more good offers that show up in your universe. I'm defining "good" offers as those that come from trusted sources and that, when you pause and let them settle a moment or two, feel fundamentally good in and to your body. (Taking that pause is an important skill in and of itself you'll develop as you practice!)

Interestingly enough, you'll notice that the act of saying yes to initial good offers will generate more delightful offers coming your way. On a practical level, people in your life will notice you can consume pleasurable things and will make you more offers.

But it's also true that you have more of something by simply having more of it.

Because pleasure capacity is indeed a muscle, let's use strength training as an example: When you lift weights, you'll find that the more weight you lift, the more weight you *can* lift. Pleasure capacity works the same way: the more you say "Yes" to pleasure and good offers, the more pleasure and good offers you'll have to say "Yes" to—thereby increasing your pleasure capacity.

Add One Thing

You can deliberately "flex" your pleasure capacity muscle by creating more experiences of pleasure.

Start by adding in one sensual element to your morning routine. For example, before leaping out of bed, pause one minute to breathe deeply and notice one thing that pleases you with one of your senses. I like to put my attention on the birds singing outside my window before I even open my eyes. Note the effect: does something now look, sound, taste, feel, or smell better? Also note how the effect resonates in your body: does having created more pleasure for yourself feel better to you?

Now, add in another element that delights one of your senses. If one or more people can experience this element with you, all the better! You're expanding your capacity to increase their pleasure as well.

Go Slowly

The old adage, "All good things in moderation," is well-suited for building pleasure capacity—and restraint is a beautiful tool to use as you develop it. Restraint may not have been the tool you were expecting here, but bear with me.

Let's say you unexpectedly receive your favorite chocolate cake from your favorite bakery. Even though the cake is delicious, you know you'll feel heavy or possibly sick if you eat more than a few slices in one sitting. If you're able to employ some restraint, you'll be able to have a pleasurable portion of a delectable thing for several days instead of consuming the whole of a good thing in one day. In this example, you've increased your pleasure by increasing the amount of time you can enjoy a thing.

Some Practical Considerations

Because I've designed a life centered on what pleases me, almost everything on my list is something I can access at a moment's notice. I make a point to keep those items readily available. It's important to remember that some aspects of your inventory will be relatively stable (I've been making and consuming chai for thirty years), while others may be more transitory (before French fries, I was into calamari).

Some items, like the chai, I purchase in bulk so I don't have to worry about running out. When my tastes shift and change, as they will, I give away my inventory and make space for something new. My pleasure is extended in the act of gifting my surplus to someone who would enjoy it. In that way, a pleasure-based lifestyle benefits others as well as oneself.

It's important to note the following: I didn't go out and get these items in one weekend; rather, I accumulated them over time. So do take your time. It probably wouldn't be pleasurable for you to gather everything that comprises your pleasure map in one go.

Also, it's completely normal for it to take a few tries before you find what products or services are most pleasing to you. I had to try out three different chai tea brands before I landed on the one that was perfect for me. Some may view multiple attempts as a waste of time and money, but I heartily disagree. Most investments worth making take a little time, patience, and yes, some money; and in this case, the investment is YOU! And yes, you are worth trying something once, twice, or more if necessary, to get it exactly the way you like it. And when you have what works for you, that feeling is so worth it.

Winning the Game of Pleasure

Finally, I want to note that the way you go about making these adjustments is every bit as important as making them. You know how it feels when someone starts barking commands as if you're doing something the wrong way? It's hard to be positively motivated to do anything for that person. Remember, this is all for you, and the process of generating more pleasure should feel…pleasurable! So have fun. Make mistakes, and chuckle as you do. When it comes to pleasurable living, the journey is everything. So, as I said in the previous chapter, hold your overall pleasure lightly, even as you pursue it with discipline and integrity.

That, friends, is how to win at the delicious game of pleasure.

Now that you have a foundation for creating pleasure in daily living at both micro and macro levels, I want to share my pleasure journey with you. From there, we'll study how to apply pleasure to the death and grieving seasons of life, since pleasure has deeply enriched those seasons in my life.

In the meantime, I look forward to hearing about your adventures in pleasure mapping; the subsequent discoveries and decisions you'll make; and the good offers you'll receive as you say, "Yes" to pleasure!

You will also enjoy this piece by Ash Canty on how the sensual aspects of simple rituals can add to your grief journey.

Ash, they/he, is a death care provider through Going with Grace. They combine death care skills with their gift of mediumship. Their hope and prayer is to bring about healing from the other side and a profound peace around life after death.

CREATING CONTAINERS FOR OUR GRIEF

In this time in which we are living, it is amazing how much we need containers for our grief as ritual. As a psychic medium, spiritual life coach, and death guide, I have learned so much from spirits in other realms on what it is to be human here on Earth. Often in mediumship readings I hear how this earthly realm is one of the most beautiful and challenging realms to be in. And a huge part of being here in this realm, they (spirits) say, is being able to live within the never-ending chasm of grief and praise. To constantly be creating and carving out moments for our grief to be felt, that is the way we will feel more, feel each other. That is how we will live more deeply and vividly.

I remember a client of mine who had just lost her mother to cancer. This woman wanted a reading to be able to connect with her mother again and see how she was; that is all I knew. In the reading, this woman's mother came through so powerfully and told me to tell her daughter, "She needed her to get inside the water and allow the grief to move." She said, "Take yourself to the river and allow yourself to feel." She also said that her daughter's grief was stuck inside her daughter's chest, which is why her daughter was having so much chest trouble.

As the message came through in the reading, this woman just stared at me, shocked. The blood drained from her face. She closed her eyes, started sobbing uncontrollably, and told me that she and her mother used to go to the river in their backyard and swim in it, and it was so powerful. She said she hadn't gone into that river since the death of her mother because she was too afraid to feel the grief. She had also become severely sick with a horrible infection in her chest soon after her mother's passing, and the doctors couldn't figure out why. This woman was so grateful to be reminded of the power of ritual and connection with the soul of her mother and this river.

I find that this kind of support from the other side happens a lot! While it is very specific for each person I am reading, there are some astounding patterns I have been noticing from spirits that help and support us to be constantly moving grief and allowing it to flow through us and not be drowned by it. There was another client of mine who got support on how to allow the sex energy work she was doing to be a healing place for her grief and to feel the pleasure within the pain. This session blew me away! Not only was this client validated by a spirit on the other side, she was also very much supported in her sex work and uplifted in the way this woman was already utilizing powerful sex work as a tool for allowing grief and praise to move through her body and be transformed.

There are hundreds of readings I have done, all with profound insight from loved ones, multidimensional beings, guides, nature beings, and more on ways to support ourselves in a grief journey.

Making time to set containers for our grief, and the grief of others, allows us to feel the bigness of our expressions as embodied spirit. In addition, we are shown that it's okay to not be okay. In fact, it's downright beautiful! There is such wisdom when we can be real with what is, and it doesn't have to be complex. All the things I offer to my clients are all things that have been shared from spirits on the other side, and they are so simple! These include activities like putting your feet in a bowl full of water and playing sad music, allowing the grief to move out of you; taking a hot bath; a variety of pleasure practices; singing, crying, dancing your body around; guttural screams; as well as getting your hands in the dirt and rubbing it all over your body!

Ritual can be so many things. It can be wild, erotic, silly, fun, sad, emotional, serious, funny, moving, deep. It can be whatever you feel deeply called to do, and it can evolve and change, just like we do. When we take a pause, come back to our bodies, back to our nervous systems, and make time to allow the grief to speak, we have so much more spaciousness within us to truly be here in this time, and not only survive but thrive within it.

Chapter 4

My Story

We'll soon apply all we're learning about pleasure to grief and dying; but I first want to share with you how pleasure came to be the critical element that shaped my adult life and my current incarnation as a death doula, and how pleasure continues to help me create a life beyond my wildest dreams. Here's my story.

The memory is like a short clip from a movie: cue the rising, earnestly fervent piano music as the camera pans a sunlit Southern California beach. It then zooms in on a young Black woman, arms raised to the sky as she exhales gleefully into the ecstasy of the morning rays bathing her naked body. Ocean waves crash before her. True bliss.

Having been raised in the aspirational culture of the Black professional middle class in L.A., I was taught to worship the hard work and sacrifice that is inherent to being part of the upwardly mobile and thoroughly oppressed sector of American society. Most anything pleasurable was viewed as a distraction from representing an entire group of people with every success and failure.

In this context, the exploration and cultivation of pleasure outside of prescribed boundaries was highly discouraged. It thus wasn't until I was in college at Seattle Pacific University, hundreds of miles away from home and isolated from traditional culture, that I was exposed to ideas about the natural world, feminism, and the sacred intersection of the two. These ideas were life-changing for me.

When I returned home after completing my Bachelor of Arts in political science, gone were the plans to attend law school. Instead, I was filled with subversive ideas of personal freedom and the sovereignty of my body.

Like many liberal arts majors, I returned home the summer after graduation essentially unemployable—except as a waitress. When a co-worker mentioned a mythical nude beach called Sacreds on the coast in the southern region of Los Angeles County near my home, I felt compelled to find it. I thought it might be a fun place to find more people who were living closer to the Earth and who enjoyed more personal freedom than anyone I knew.

I failed to locate the beach based on my coworker's sketchy directions; but I did happen upon a couple on an adjacent beach who brought me directly to it. It turned out that Sacreds was surrounded by cliffs and required a quarter-mile hike down a steep, worn path—which contributed to its privacy. You had to really want to be there, and I would later discover that the people who came down regularly were fiercely protective of each other, and especially protective of the women.

The next time I traveled to the beach, I found it easily, and with the exception of one person off on the far side of the beach, I had it all to myself. I sat for a few minutes on my towel, simply taking in the beauty of my surroundings and the sound of the waves crashing to shore. When I felt ready, I walked out to the edge of the water...and then, almost without thinking about it, I slipped out of my dress, and the sun kissed my body for the first time. The moment was shattering and liberating and ancient and true. I became embodied.

And then, counter to all of what my conditioning had trained me to believe…nothing bad happened. There was just the sun, the sand, the sea, and me and my body. For the rest of the summer, when I wasn't waiting tables, I was on that relatively secluded nude beach soaking up the sun and conversation among the regulars who exposed me to new ways of thinking and being.

Because there was a shortage of teachers in Los Angeles County, I obtained an emergency teaching credential and began teaching middle school English in the fall. My memory of my time on the beach lingered, but I decided it was time to focus on adulting. So, over the course of the next three years, I continued teaching and got married. And then, with my husband, I moved to Seattle to get a master's degree in Organization Development from Seattle Pacific University.

Something, though, was missing. My classes were going well enough, but they weren't filling…*something*—a nameless need I had. And my marriage, which was never great, was slowly disintegrating. I found a group called "Diving Deep and Resurfacing," which was based around a book by feminist writer Carol Patrice Christ. The premise of the group (and book) was that by diving consciously into your sorrow and pain, you could re-emerge with a reclaimed sense of yourself; and the idea of doing that work in the exclusive company of women was new to me and offered safety and resonance.

We met every other week for three months. There were eight women in the group, plus two group leaders, who helped us communicate honestly about where we were. Through several embodied activities—like guided meditation, journaling, ritual, and walks in nature—they created a solid container that allowed us to safely explore the soft, rich power of the stuff of the shadow (the hard stuff) and the feminine.

This class imparted to me the valuable practice of keeping sensual things in one's space—things that spoke to all of one's senses, such as candles, music, fragrant oils, and the like—that elicited a sense of grounded beauty and well-being. This practice remains an integral part of my pleasure practice.

I finished my graduate program a year later and moved to the San Francisco Bay Area for a job at Hewlett Packard. I was still married and still focused on my career—it takes time to undo society's definitions of success and happiness, after all! Nonetheless, I was still using the tools I'd learned in my women's group: occasional nature walks and bath salts, candles, and fresh flowers.

And don't underestimate the power of such simple, sensual tools, friends: they were doing their work on me. I was going to work every day at Hewlett Packard, but those bath salts and such were continuing to help me uncover who I really was. Also, this was all occurring during the time of my Saturn return. Gradually, the realization was dawning that my goals were changing. I was no longer compelled to orient my life around who other people thought I should be but rather the kind of woman that I wanted to be.

As this new point of view took hold, I departed the familiar path and left my career and my husband behind as I started another graduate program and another women's group, one that met monthly for nine months. This one was very earth-based and ritually focused on eco-feminism. It was full of all kinds of sensual exercises designed to help us reclaim our feminine bodies. We harnessed the power of our connection to the earth to fuel our ability to re-imagine our lives. It was an extraordinary class, one that ignited all our senses. I'm still friends with some of those women.

This work intersected beautifully with the study of psychotherapy at the California Institute of Integral Studies in San Francisco. What a fun romp! I moved into a studio apartment overlooking the beach and immersed myself in a lovely season of reclamation and self-exploration.

Eventually, though, I needed more income. I left the beach scene and returned to work at Hewlett Packard for a few years and then eventually landed at Levi Strauss. It turned out the company was in the midst of a cultural shift, so there wasn't much work for me to do. Intellectual stimulation and personal growth came in the form of workshops I was taking in my off-hours in the area of meditation and spirituality, which eventually led me to Lafayette Morehouse.

And so began my twenty-year study of responsible hedonism.

ཨ ཨ ཨ

It was in this context that I discovered what some might call "the secret to happiness," which is remarkably simple: *Look around your world and focus on what makes you feel good.*

In other words: put your attention on your life, and find the things in it that exist right now that gratify you, that make you happy, that make you feel good. This action is all the more important if you have little that makes you feel good; for the act itself, your attention itself on what *is* feeling good, expands that very feeling.

And here's what I learned about happiness: it's much more inclusive than we've been taught. Real happiness actually includes life *and* death, sorrow *and* joy, the fabulous *and* the dumb shit. It includes the mess of real life. Welcomes it, actually. Embraces it. And real life, yours and mine, is all happening right now.

By embracing it, you're taking responsibility for it on some level. Once you claim responsibility, you have the power of creation. The current dominant culture into which many of us were born, and which we inhale daily, wants you to think happiness can't include "right now." It tells you that *after* you have better clothes, a more svelte shape, a younger face, a better job, more money, a gorgeous partner, and 2.5 perfect children living in a huge house in the best neighborhood, then, *then!,* you'll be happy. The only problem is, this faux happiness requires that you never stop getting more— more and better clothes, a leaner body, an ever-younger face—and God forbid your huge house ever gets messy.

The truth is, you get to say when you're happy, when it's enough. More importantly, you—and only you—get to say what makes you happy. Not because you're settling but because you are truly gratified by what you have presently and have some ideas about what might gratify you next.

On the playground of this experimental community, I learned that happiness meant pursuing a life that actually gratified *me*. A life that *I* actually wanted.

༓ ༓ ༓

Discovering what pleased me took some time. This is because figuring out what you actually want versus what society tells you you *should* want, means confronting yourself. Your true self.

I started by writing in my journal. Just writing my thoughts as if no one would ever read them. I also asked people I trusted to tell me when I seemed happiest.

And periodically, I'd pause, turn my gaze inward, and ask myself, "What do I want?" In the beginning, I had to develop discernment. After writing down my first response, I'd ask the question again, and I'd answer again for a total of four times.

Here's what an answer for me may have looked like:

I'd like to go to the pool now.
It would be even more fun to have a couple friends join me.
And wouldn't it be great if we had some music and snacks.
Yes, that is what I want.
That would make me happy right now.

In this particular moment, here is what happiness feels like: a beautiful cup of coffee in my hands as I sit on my sofa with my dogs at my feet.

What would make it even better would be some music.

So, I've just turned some on. Now, I'm even happier. Even more pleasured.

※ ※ ※

Two years ago, I found out my mother was dying. I wasn't ready. But I applied all I'd learned along the way, and I made the experience gratifying for my mother, my brother, and myself by looking around our world, noticing what was feeling good to us (which I could discern from practice) and leaning into that.

After my mom passed, I began a new inquiry: How can a person—myself, in this case—grieve well? Grieve pleasurably?

I discovered that what felt good to me was to feel the grief in my body, *through* my body, which I'll explore more in the next chapter.

However, I'll say this: the tools I used weren't new to me. I'd learned them on the nude beach, in my women's groups, in my psychotherapy classes, dozens of workshops, and living in community. They simply were re-purposed for this moment in my life. And they were effective. I was able to ground myself in my body as I was grieving, experiencing my body as a good place, safe space, as I witnessed tremendous emotion roiling through it. And I was able to embrace the experience, as sorrowful as it was, with some amount of awe and joy. Because if you can ground yourself in your own body, and thus, in your own experience, you will discover, as I did, that even within deep sorrow and grief, joy is there, too.

Even through the pandemic and a move from California to Washington, I continued to grow my vocation as a midwife of sorts in the realm of death and grief, from a pleasure-based perspective. For just as pleasure is a most honorable and helpful orientation in life, so it is the same in death and grieving.

Sometimes when I go outside and take in the gorgeous view of the trees in the back yard, I remember the young Black woman who raised her arms to the sky all those years ago on that nude beach, and I luxuriate in the morning rays caressing my skin the way she did, as the ocean waves sang their song of celebration, seemingly all for her.

And I know I fulfilled her dream. To know herself. To *be* herself. To be evermore embodied. True bliss.

༔ ༔ ༔

Exercise #1: Ask yourself, "What do I want?" And then, ask three more times. You may be surprised by your answer.

Exercise #2: Take a look around your world at any given moment and see if you can find one thing that gratifies you right then. Take a bit of time to claim it, own it, wallow in it. And then continue with your day. Or you can find the next thing. Try it for a few days and notice what happens.

Chapter 5

Pleasure Applied to Dying and Grieving

Now you understand a bit more about my own personal pleasure journey, and how my mother's death led to the discovery that pleasure is the critical factor, which elevates grief and dying to their rightful, sacred, and yes, even at times profoundly joyful status—right alongside all other emotions and life transitions.

Next, we will explore why pleasure is an alchemizing, gentle, and natural component within grief and dying, one that can make both experiences healing and expansive; and I'll share how deliberately incorporating pleasure profoundly impacted my mother, my family, and me while she (my mother) was dying.

Reframing Death and Grief

By now, you have some understanding that pleasure is more than candles and soft music. The courageous practice of actually feeling the world you occupy enough to know what creates more of that elevated state through thoughts and actions—it's life-changing work.

So, imagine applying that skill to the end of life…or as it may be more aptly called, another major life transition. Doing so, though, requires a reframe of this passage from one generally associated with decline to one that is actually a doorway into something new. When perceived this way, the tools of pleasure help you claim life to the very end rather than reduce this part of life to something to be avoided at all costs.

The first step is to reexamine our perception of death and grief. The standard societal narrative surrounding these life events—that affect everyone, by the way—is to freak out that something bad and downright abnormal is happening, when in fact, what is happening is a completely normal physiological and mental function. What's true is that all physical forms, our bodies included, will change, and thus, at some point, will cease to exist in their current forms. To be alive is to be in a constant state of change.

White supremacist capitalism supports change in only one direction: growth, expansion, bigger, more. In contrast, biological life ebbs and flows, rises and falls, expands and contracts. Being in a state of dynamic change is how living systems thrive. Leaning too heavily in one direction creates imbalance and threatens the continued existence of a living system. The human body is comprised of dynamic systems and belongs to other, greater configurations as well. It's entirely fallacious to apply a theoretical economic model to living systems. Yet, the medical industrial complex—which impacts so much of our health and death care—does exactly that with relentless fanaticism.

If, however, we replace the capitalist lens with a more humanistic one (which would make a great deal more sense, since we're actually talking about humans), then it's easy to remember that the natural cycle of being in a human body is to be conceived, be born, grow and change, and then die. When death and grief are given their proper place in the natural flow of life, it makes sense that a life lived pleasurably would include death and grief experienced graciously as well.

In fact, attention on what could feel good to the dying and their kin during such important transitions could only enhance the process for everyone involved. Imagine a death that shifted the focus from merely alleviating suffering to something of a higher order. This shift would actually elevate the process.

Before the Civil War, people in many cultures around the world typically died at home surrounded by loved ones. After death, the bodies were washed with care and prepared for burial on a remote section of home land or at sea. Returning to this slower, more humane process, which likely took into account what would make the transition more pleasant, is a return to rituals that humans have enacted for centuries and that many continue to practice today.

Making My Mother's Death Pleasurable

When my mother was dying, I took care to make her transition as pleasant for her as possible. I studied what made her life enjoyable for her when she was healthy, and I made sure those factors were a part of her dying process as well. To that end, she was always covered in her faux mink blanket. My mother had the TV on 24 hours a day most of her life, and so we left it on as much as possible through her active dying process. I knew she wanted certain gospel music playing as she was dying, so we played it intermittently.

My mother loved live music and concerts, so we scheduled an acapella choir, a harpist, and a soloist to perform at her bedside at different times.

In the domain of spirituality, I made sure that a minister from the AME church visited during the vigil. My mother wasn't very religious throughout most of her life, but during her final years, she started attending a Bible study class to my great surprise and my brother's delight. A couple years earlier, I'd had a casual conversation with her about her final wishes, during which she indicated that she wanted an AME minister at her bedside. It was soul-nourishing to have him there, because his presence elicited some delightful stories from my brother and me from our life with our mother. Talkin' story is a good use of the sixth sense, which can also be described as conceptual thought.

While all of these sensual elements were customized to what we knew my mother would enjoy, they also proved to be an emotional and physical comfort to us, her family. Holding her hand through the sorrow of losing her was made sweeter by having contact with the incredible softness of the faux fur, for example.

We also ate as well as we wanted, and we gave each other breaks. When I wasn't at my mother's bedside, I intentionally fortified myself with experiences that delighted my senses as a way to increase my capacity for compassion. I would watch light comedies on TV or have conversations with extended family members who were especially supportive and good company. Some friends left a bouquet of flowers on my dining room table one evening, and there was that moment when I stood outside in the field and just took in the stars for a few minutes, imagining that my beautiful mother would be joining them soon.

Perhaps it sounds callous or selfish that I sought out enjoyment during such a sorrowful time for my mother and family. However, those activities are familiar from my ordinary life. Why should the journey of dying and grieving be so different? In fact, all I'm really doing here is consciously naming these acts as pieces of a process that could feel good and be supportive.

Seeking out delight is an important aspect of a death vigil. This is because *people who are gratified have more space to be generous than people who are depleted.* They have more capacity for compassion and generosity, which is a useful space to be in when one enters the mysterious realm of active dying. Being in a state of gratification allows you to be present to the majesty that is available when someone exits the realm of the living. And you wouldn't want to miss that.

This same capacity is also useful for grieving. I have already written about how the use of the senses can support the process of grieving. Here, though, I want to emphasize how effective it can be to approach your own grief with kindness and an open mind.

For me, after the initial shock wore off, I came to see the universal experience I was having as an opportunity to explore an entirely new set of feelings and experiences. Eschewing the hater in my head that tried to call me out for holding myself "too precious," I deliberately closed myself off a bit from the rest of the world. It turns out that this is not hard to do because many people feel awkward around folks who are in mourning anyway.

I specifically chose those I let in—my support team—based on who could be available to the full range of expression and the possibility of pleasure in the grief process. I also had the luxury of time as the coronavirus pandemic ensued.

What became evident almost immediately was how much relief there was in a good cry. Shimmers would course through my body, and I would deliberately continue to sob until I got all the way down to the bottom of the feeling. In the end, I was wrung out but lighter. Following up a cry fest with a walk in the park would feel gratifying, as the acuity of my senses were expanded. I could feel the natural world hold me as I celebrated the breeze on my face, the sunlight on the trees, the delicious smell of wet earth or bay laurels, the music of birds. The walking created the space for me to integrate where I had just been on my path into sorrow and the gems of understanding that came from letting it unfold. The moving and feeling myself in the physical world allowed for the integration of the sorrow together with the lush aspects of life. After a walk, I would come home and have a cup of chai and talk easily with whomever was around.

By allowing the space to have my grief process fully and pleasurably through my body—in other words, sensually—I developed a greater ability to access a full range of emotions and experience. When I had trouble focusing, as soon as I noticed, I would chuckle to myself and say, "Ah, grief!" Then I would take a break, short or long, and do something that didn't require focused attention, like listen to a podcast or make a yummy snack or just daydream. That was on a good day.

There were many times I just wandered in circles metaphorically for hours, or I'd doubt myself, wondering whether I was becoming senile because I couldn't remember simple stuff. All that happened, too. That's how my grief manifested. When I'd catch myself in this unhelpful pattern, I'd invariably chuckle and quietly forgive myself and then get back to the sacred work of holding space for my grief in whatever ways felt especially good to me. Sound baths, breathwork, meditation, and walks were among my favorite activities.

Honestly, it just felt better in both my body and soul to confront grief rather than avoid it. Releasing the stagnate emotional places felt especially good because energy and inspiration became quickly available on the other side of them.

The Current State of Grief Management

What I'm proposing is very different from how the dominant culture approaches grief. If you're lucky, you get a couple days off work and then you're expected to get right back to it. Full immersion in the hustle and grind is the expectation in a culture that clearly doesn't value life, so how could it possibly take death into account?

With no training and insufficient communication around death, friends and family fall in line with the dominant paradigm of the hustle and grind. They largely ignore the fact that death has occurred in preference for a supposed return to the "land of the living," which isn't really living at all. Perhaps within their subconscious lies the awareness that if they spent any time contemplating the life that just passed into oblivion, or even their own life after a significant loss of a loved one, they might discover they haven't really been living at all. And that realization could lead to serious disruption of a status quo, which depends on people steadfastly avoiding death and the resulting grief so that they can continue avoiding life in service to the economic machine of capitalism.

Thus, it is that we return to work within a day or two of a loved one dying, and a few people offer superficial condolences the first day, and then it's never mentioned again after that unless there is a "dysfunction" of some sort. Family and friends do the same, sending cards and flowers up until the funeral, and then afterwards, life is expected to get back to normal. Spending barely any time with the enormity or *majesty* of the loss, we're expected to get back to our regular life without missing a beat. And we do, as this premature return is the only way to remain part of the mainstream economic and social engines.

The R(evolution) of Death Care

I mentioned earlier that it used to be that people died at home. Then they started dying in hospitals, and we left all the muss and fuss to the professionals, because after all, what did we know? At the beginning of the twentieth century, more people dying of natural causes died at home. The 1950s is when more people began dying in the hospital, and that trend continued growing through the end of the century, according to recent research.

The only problem is that hospitals are where people go to get better. These institutions are oriented around keeping people physically alive as long as possible. What with the harsh lighting and constant drone of beeps and voices, it turns out they are not necessarily the best places for dying

Surprisingly, hospitals are now starting to send people home to die—it probably has something to do with a balance sheet. It's also true that more people have seen what happened to their parents dying in hospitals and are opting to die at home instead. However, you're not guaranteed a better experience there, either. The problem with dying at home is that only the rich can afford the kind of skilled medical care required to make that a comfortable experience for the person dying while not burning out the 1-2 family members typically tasked with caregiving.

Wherever someone is dying, though, it's possible to have it be as pleasurable as possible. For starters, most medical and hospice care providers, as well as family members, are most likely doing their level-best to make the dying person comfortable.

However, the revolution—or evolution—of death care begins with this thought: Even with the dying person's pain being managed and being positioned in a comfortable bed surrounded by flowers and cards, *there is still room to add in something more that would be pleasing!*

Bringing the Tenets of a Pleasure Practice to Death Care

As I've stated in my previous chapters, the most important tenet of a pleasure practice is asking, given what you know, what would make the current experience feel even better.

Of course, when you're looking to bring pleasure to someone else, it's always better to start by asking him/her/them this question. I've said before that there are many social and personal reasons why someone would not be able—or willing—to respond to a straightforward question, like, "Is there anything I can get you that would delight you right now?" In that case, you can bring everything you know about them and/or the current situation to mind and then make them a couple of offers in the realm of the five senses. For example:

"Would you like to listen to some gospel music?"

"Would you like to have your feet rubbed for a few minutes?

"Can I get you a chocolate chip cookie from the kitchen or the cafeteria?

"I have a video of your niece. Would you like to see it?"

Notice that each of these offers is specific. In the realm of pleasure, it's best to ask specific yes/no questions because they require the least amount of effort in terms of a response. If the person says no, then at least you have more information. However, rather than responding with, "Well, what DO you want?", you can just keep asking specific questions until you arrive at the destination: something they actually want. It's very likely they will either agree to your offer or counter with something they do want, now that you've got them thinking about something that would please them.

Of course, if they do respond to your very first question with a specific request, then do what they ask as soon as it is possible to do so. If the request is for something that is not in the realm of possibilities, like flying off to a foreign country, then you can use a bit of creativity and make your best counter-offer. You could suggest a travelog from YouTube of the country, or the next time you visit you could bring some food from the country.

Here's an example of how this kind of conversation might go:

> *Caregiver:* Can I get you a chocolate chip cookie from the kitchen or the cafeteria?
> *Person:* No, thanks.
> *Caregiver:* Okay. Can I get you a cherry popsicle?
> *Person:* Nope. I'm really not hungry.
> *Caregiver:* I've been reading a delightful novel by Terry McMillian. Can I read to you a bit?

Person: Oh, I remember that movie about how somebody got their groove back. It reminded me of this romance I had on vacation in Hawaii years ago. Yes! Read me some Terry.

As you can see, this dialogue can become a rich conversation to have with someone in the final weeks or months of their life. It's a level up in tone from adjusting their pillows or administering medications. It's also more substantive than soft music, flowers, and candles. *What people want at the end of their lives is to be truly seen.* That could mean leaving them alone to sleep or watch a movie. It could also mean having someone around who is paying enough attention to make a remarkable and sometimes scary journey a bit more sweet.

If the person can no longer speak, then you simply have to use your best judgement given everything you know about them and what could make anyone feel better in the circumstance. Don't be afraid to ask someone who you think has more information than you, either. Your question may get rebuffed if a loved one is feeling particularly emotional at the moment of the inquiry, but it's better to ask than to not, for a variety of reasons.

First, they probably have some good information. Second, your inquiry could spark joy or open the field to other possibilities of experience beyond sorrow and suffering. And it could also become an opportunity of some unforeseeable benefit that you may never know, or at best, will learn about later.

In any case, the process of making the final phase of life more pleasurable allows you to become the kind of companion in death who is uplifting to the person dying, and most likely other folks in the vicinity, and most importantly to yourself. Pleasure is just the context. What's actually happening is that relationships are forming and deepening. And that's a gift you can keep long after the person is no longer here physically.

Pleasure for the Caretakers and Grievers

A pleasure-oriented approach is also very helpful for the family and/or loved ones who are or will be grieving and/or attending the dying—you, included. From my point of view, family members, especially caregivers, do not get enough attention and support. Making pleasurable offers to the very people doing the emotional and often physical heavy lifting associated with being with someone actively dying is a kindness that cannot be underestimated in its value and contribution to the overall process of dying.

For example, it's one thing to give a family caregiver a respite; it's quite another, though, to arrange a massage for them during their time off. I've heard of caregivers getting treated to beautiful meals and live music events and outdoor adventures like hikes or fishing. The pleasure doesn't even have to be costly or time intensive. It could be something as simple as casually asking them about foods they enjoy and serving them a special snack outside on the porch; running them a hot bath at the end of a long care shift; or cueing up a rom-com on Netflix with an actor you've heard them mention.

It could even be as simple as looking them in the eyes and genuinely asking how they are *actually* doing, then allowing them the space to do an emotional download, or giving them a five-minute shoulder or foot rub.

If you get stuck for ideas, initiate a conversation with them and keep the six senses in mind to see whether there is anything they reveal that would please them in any of those realms.

Here's a list of some pleasurable activities that will get you thinking about what might work for you and/or your loved ones. Discover your own practices by just noting in any given day some instances when something feels good to you. It could be a mental note, or you could write it down for further exploration. By writing it down, you stand a better chance of recalling it when you need it. It's also a great way to get to know yourself and begin custom crafting a world that really suits you.

Grief gives you that permission like no other.

Pleasure Practices:

Walking in nature
Your favorite beverage (being careful not to overdo alcohol)
Music that reminds or soothes or validates
Grief counseling
A nourishing meal from your favorite restaurant
Watching your favorite movie that uplifts you
Real conversations with people you trust
The healing arts—bodywork, reiki, acupuncture, etc.
All the stuff that makes you smile and feel happy to be alive
Do what you want to do

This practice of leveling up from comfort to pleasure might seem like it takes significant time and energy. The trick, though, is to do only what you actually want to do, and nothing more. Do not make any offers that would tax you in any way to give or perform. Acts that are performed grudgingly or with any amount of stress are not going to add as much good as the ones that are given freely and with a bit of delight.

Pleasure is not about sacrifice. That's actually called service. There's nothing wrong with service. There is definitely a place for that. Remember, though, we're talking about situations where the basic needs and comforts have been met, and this is a bit of icing on the cake. Truly, this should be as fun to give as it is for the other person to receive. That's how you reach an elevated state.

For example, I spent some time with a client who had just finished a long visit with her son. He'd wanted to reconcile some events from his childhood. I brought her water, re-positioned her in bed, and then dimmed the lights so she could rest. Before I left, I turned on some music an old friend of hers had recorded so she could drift off to sleep with the sound of her friend singing her to sleep.

Another example was bringing my brother some takeout from a favorite restaurant of his so that he would have something better than cafeteria food to eat when he got home after his vigil shift.

In both instances, it brightened my own mood to perceive the joy both recipients were experiencing. Putting that kind of good in their world added to the good in mine. Therein lies the secret of providing pleasure to others: *pleasure truly offered is pleasure experienced by everyone involved.* There's nothing sacrificial or altruistic about it. If you are paying enough attention to give someone something they truly want, and it's not costing you more than you want to give, then it can add to the good in your world, too, as you get to experience the joy that results from giving pleasure.

Pleasure Benefits Everyone

Making a point to feel good while providing death care or grieving, and/or making a point to ensure the dying person feels good during this life transition—in other words, making these processes pleasurable—benefits everyone. The dominant culture will tell you that doing this is selfish. However, if you'll consider a pleasure-centric grieving and dying process through a lens that values people over production, and if you will let the ideas in this chapter settle, you might feel the rightness of them, their resonance, in your body. This is because pleasure is the natural human state. We are our best, truest, and most generous selves when we lead pleasure-centric lives.

In my next chapter, I'll provide a step-by-step guide for dying people and their loved ones to make the experience as pleasure-centric as possible instead of merely comfort-centric. While I've shared some possibilities in this chapter, I want to provide structured guidance that will enable you to more fully honor yourself and your loved ones during times of grief and dying.

In the meantime, I'd like to offer the perspective of Melanie DeMore on the power of music, specifically song, in the last phase of life.

Melanie is a vocal activist. She has been called to the bedsides of both newborns and those in transition. She has chanted and toned to awaken the newcomer into this world, and soothed many a weary soul about to pass, with praises and hymns for a life well lived.

The following is an edited conversation I had with Melanie in February 2022, on her experience singing at bedsides during the active phase of dying.

M: I'm one of the close friends of the founder of the Threshold Choir [Kate Munger]. I have a very unique position in Threshold. I get to work with all the choirs. For most of them, and there's over 230 of them now, one of the first songs they learned is "Sending You Light." So, it is a staple. Every choir all over the world knows that song.

On holding vigil for her younger sister, Drina, who was dying of multiple sclerosis.

M: You know, people would come and go and all that, but I noticed what happens between here and there. When Drina was letting go of that corporeal body, her arms and her legs were moving. She's lying down on her back, something she could not do, and her legs are moving. It's like she was just dancing in between *here* and *there*.

There's that letting go of the thing that tethers you down to where your spirit begins to expand itself and lift out. I've seen that a number of times. For some folks, it can be really scary—like, what is going on? What we're talking about is going beyond this.

I also knew in my time there with Drina, when I needed to leave the room. You have to listen to these things if you're going to be at bedside. You have to be awake and attuned. And you have to be still so that you can see these things, and understand. If you're going to tend to somebody, you need your intuition. You have to know when to step back. When to leave that space. When to stop singing and not speak.

Part of the work of being at bedside is to know when to step back. When I worked with the Threshold Choir, Kate developed a whole bunch of hand signals that they could see so that there's no [extra chatter]. You have to be able to just really flow because none of it is predictable. You have to be willing to serve.

With Drina, songs would just come, and I would just sing them for her. As you are singing, what's important is that the sound and the words land over there in her expanding space. In fact, I would regulate whatever I was singing to her breathing pattern.

She loved ice skating, and that's what it was like when she was in between *here* and *there*. It was like she was just gliding. It was amazing. Now limbs are moving that had not been moving. She could not move her legs when she was *here*, but between *here* and *there*, she's moving and rolling from one side of her body to the next with her arms. It was extraordinary. That is the thing about between *here* and *there*.

I actually wrote a song called "Here and There." It's a circular kind of thing, and it moves with you. I'm here. I'm here. *[Finger in the air pointing downward, moving in a circular pattern, and then another finger a little higher pointing downward, moving in a circular pattern.]* And so you're hearing they're *here*, and they're hearing that you are *here* and *there*, like that. And dying has other parts so that there are these different levels with *here* and *there*.

So, you have all these different parts. When you put them all together, there's all this movement because it was miraculous to watch that, to feel her ascending, expanding.

You also have to be so much out of the way to know the right thing to do. When the funeral people came and got her, I walked her body to the ambulance, and I'm singing

"Gilead" the whole way because she loved that song. I also knew my family loved that song.

I've sung for lots of people. I've sung for folks on the phone who are in the hospital. I don't have any preconceived notion as to what I'm going to sing. Sometimes it's just something that comes out at the time.

When I'm talking with folks about singing at bedside, I say, first of all, it's not like singing as you think. It has nothing to do with performance in any way. It has everything to do with the intention. It is egoless, which is hard for us to do sometimes. There are a lot of brilliant singers in the world, but not all of them can sing at bedside because it's not a solo enterprise, even if you're singing by yourself. I talked with them about how you have to understand the power of music and song, and about blending with the people that you're singing with. It's entirely vibrational.

And it's different if you're singing by yourself because it's just you. But if you are singing with other people, you've got to be in tune with each other, and that's not just musically. You gotta be in tune with the person dying.

O: When I discovered this at my father's bedside, I was just adding a vibration to the vibration that had just kind of opened up into the room and felt like it wanted to be met.

M: So, the thing is that vibration is always there. It's interesting how things will realign in ways that we are just not even aware of, and yet that's the thing I was saying earlier about knowing when to leave the room because you need to take your energy. It makes more room for that process to happen.

It's not complicated. Why does a kid cry when they've hurt themselves or hum when they're upset? Because it vibrates on a cellular level and reconnects you with all the stuff we've been talking about [that all this is life, and life includes death]. The voice, a song, just anchors us into the truth of everything.

Chapter 6

Bringing It All Together

So, we've examined why pleasure is a critical factor in a well-lived life and a lovingly orchestrated death.

Here, now, is a step-by-step guide for dying people, their caretakers, and their loved ones that will explain how to elevate the dying and death experience from comfort-centric to pleasure-centric. While I've shared some possibilities for how to undertake this process throughout this book, I now want to provide structured, practical instruction that will enable anyone to more fully honor themselves and their loved ones while dying, caretaking, and/or grieving.

Note: Out of a desire to respect and represent everyone's gender identity, I have varied the use of feminine, masculine, and nonbinary pronouns within this section.

What Death Care Can Be

Today's current model of caring for the dying is comfort-centric. Spiritual and psychological workers tend to the emotional comfort of the dying person. Medical teams and caregivers make the patient as physically comfortable as possible via hospital equipment, pain remediation, and body care, which includes meals, bathing, etc. With this model of care, for instance, if a dying patient complains of a bed sore, then the caregiver would provide salve, a bandage, and a change in positioning.

The point of comfort-centric deathcare is to ensure the dying person is in as little pain as possible. A noble and vitally important and compassionate goal, yes; but with pleasure-centric death care, we can focus further than the objective of pain reduction. We can aim for the dying person—and her caregivers—to *feel as good as possible throughout the death process.*

For example, if a dying patient complains of a bed sore under the auspices of pleasure-centric care, in addition to the standard treatment, the caregiver may implement gel cushion pillows for pressure point relief, as that addition might increase the person's pleasure while resting. Or, perhaps he would be re-positioned more frequently and more gently; and perhaps that experience would be enhanced with some aromatherapy or music.

Thus, not only is the patient now more comfortable but he feels good as well.

The Benefits of Pleasure-Centric Death Care

While the comfort-centric model of death care carries tremendous value, further advancement to the pleasure-centric model ensures even more gains.

A helpful starting point is understanding pleasure as an energy source, a source of fuel. I think it may be the purest fuel on the planet. Thus, more felt pleasure creates more energy, more buoyancy, so that a dying person can more nimbly navigate the many vicissitudes of that process. When we have more pleasure-based energy in our bodies, we are empowered—we literally have more power—to handle difficulties with greater grace.

For example, my client, Francesca, without warning was rendered immobile by her illness and needed to move from her bedroom with its standard bed to another room in the house that had a hospital bed, which would better accommodate her new needs. We could have transported her through the house, as that mode of transfer would have been the fastest and most efficient. Instead, we settled her into her wheelchair and, via an external door in her old room, brought her outside and around the long way of the house. This route took more time, yes; but as she transferred rooms, she could feel the warm, dusky air on her skin and see the finished result of a new project in the yard that had been completed just for her.

With that additional consideration, what could've been a painful transfer became a magical trip through a part of her home that was her pride and joy, and which, it turned out, she would never see again. The smile on Francesca's face and the lightness in her countenance conveyed the satisfaction of that simple decision to take the more pleasurable route.

Pleasure-centric death care also creates more pleasant memories for loved ones. When they and caretakers can plan and then either witness or partake with the dying person in pleasure-based activities, loved ones have more to hold on to, more wonderful things to remember about their dying loved one, right up to the end. It can be a great comfort to know your beloved experienced joy in their last days—and that you were a part of it.

Finally, the dying person can actively create the kind of death they want. Even if we, as a culture, don't want to think about dying, everyone wants to have a good death. With some thought, it becomes possible to include additional elements in the journey that will ensure that very outcome. Whether it's someone to listen to (or even capture) the beloved's stories; or attune the environment for their delight in the form of a favorite blanket or plants; or simply being a silent, spacious presence, this level of decision-making and planning can make for an experience of dying that is graciously curated for each individual.

Caregivers, too, benefit from pleasure-centric caregiving. This model creates more resilience—not in the sense of being strong, but rather the capacity to nurture oneself well enough to come back to the work refreshed and more vibrant and creative than before. Think in this case of resilience as a reed that bends but doesn't break. And greater resilience lends itself to greater generosity and compassion, too.

"Pleasure and Dying Shouldn't Go Together."

Before we talk about pleasure-centric grief care, I want to pause here and address a roadblock I often encounter.

After I describe to new clients and their loved ones and caregivers my process for death care, I am sometimes greeted with some uncomfortable silences. Finally, one brave soul admits that for some reason, it just feels *wrong* to focus on pleasure when someone is dying. "Pleasure and dying," she says, "just don't feel right going together."

Here is my response:

"Pleasure," I say, "is not the focus of how I do death care. Pleasure-centric death care is more about the *way* one can do all the parts of dying, the way you go about the process."

In other words, pleasure-centric death care includes everything you already need to do to create comfort; but it means doing all of that *through a sensual lens*—a lens that focuses on what feels good bodily, via the senses of touch, sound, smell, taste, sight, and thought. This lens allows for additional opportunities to elevate the experience for the person dying, the caregivers, and the grieving survivors, too.

Creating a Pleasure-Centric Death for Your Dying Loved One

Now that we've addressed the resistance to pleasure-centric death care, let's discuss the basics of making a dying loved one's process pleasure-centric.

The very first and most important step is to *put your attention on the person who is dying and consider what aspects of their past and current life brought them delight.*

To borrow a prompt from Marie Kondo, what would spark joy for her? Write down everything you know or can remember that would bring joy to the person. Remember, you can always check with additional friends and loved ones.

Keep in mind that what brought him pleasure before might not have the same effect now. For example, perhaps your loved one loves reading science fiction but is experiencing a loss of eyesight. It's possible that the slight modification of reading aloud could still produce the pleasurable experience of consuming a story. As always, though, it's best to discuss modifications with your beloved beforehand.

It's also important to keep paying attention so you can notice when whatever is happening no longer feels as good as it did a couple moments ago—and this always happens at some point!—so that you can make adjustments or discontinue. Here's an example of how this kind of adjustment might occur.

Typically, the dying person will need to have some kind of food on their stomach to take their meds. You could just give them whatever is convenient, but why not provide something they enjoy? I had a client who was really enjoying buttered toast with strawberry jam as she took her meds. We made sure her favorite strawberry jam was always on hand. She soon grew tired of it, though, and so we changed to a certain type of saltine she enjoyed until she could no longer eat at all. At that point, we tended more to her other senses that still allowed her to experience pleasure—playing her dearly loved jazz albums and ensuring fresh air and soft lighting.

A final note: once you've completed this initial and critical step of *putting your attention on the dying person and considering what aspects of their past and current life brought him delight,* you can always go back and fine tune and do a bit of editing—discontinuing this adjustment, adding in that new one that suits current conditions. The tastes and perceptions of the person dying will change in some ways—more than you might imagine.

Yoko Sen has made a significant contribution to end-of-life medical care by advocating for more pleasurable soundscapes in medical facilities.

Here is an excerpt from "The Sounds of Healing" article by Michaela Hass for Reasons to be Cheerful. Be sure to read her book, *Bouncing Forward: The Art and Science of Cultivating Resilience.*

> *What Washington musician Yoko Sen describes as the "soundtrack of her life" is not one of the songs she wrote for the band* Dust Galaxy, *but the alarm*

of the heart monitor at her hospital bedside. "The constant rhythm of a cardiac monitor ticking like a time bomb reminded me every second that my life is finite," she says.

Sen, who speaks with a very gentle, soft voice, seems to have been born with an uncanny sensitivity for music. She begged her mother for piano lessons when she was only three years old. The piano teacher told her mother to bring her daughter back when she was five, but Sen kept insisting. A picture shows the little girl on the stool in front of a grand piano, her feet far above the pedals. After moving from Japan to the U.S. in 1999, she continued her career as a professional ambient electronic musician, toured with her electro band Dust Galaxy *and published solo albums.*

When the U.S.-based Japanese artist fell ill in 2012 and had to spend weeks in hospitals, she found the jarring sounds there detrimental to her healing. "I thought it was torture, the cacophony of alarms, beeps, doors slamming, the squeaking of carts, people screaming, yellow alarm, red alarm, Code Blue." At the time, it wasn't clear if Sen would make a full recovery. She was connected to four different machines, and each emitted a different sound. Her sensitive ears were especially bothered by the constant beeping of her heart monitor. "It was a C note, and in the distance I heard high-pitched beeps when somebody fell out of bed — an F sharp, and I felt as if the sounds amplified my fear and feelings of helplessness."

Sen recognized the so-called tritone. "In medieval times, it was known as the devil's interval," an unsettling tonal dissonance that used to be banned in churches. Jimi Hendrix wrote it into his intro to "Purple Haze," Wagner into his Götterdämmerung, and film composers often use it to announce impending doom. Our bodies involuntarily respond to the dissonance with tension and unease. So why use such sounds in a place of healing?

At the beginning of her research, Sen first did what a musician does best: listen. "How about we ask the people who have to listen to these sounds every day?" she said. She and her husband, Avery Sen, an innovation researcher, interviewed hundreds of patients, nurses and doctors. "We first tried to understand, because you don't just show up with a solution," Sen says about the ensuing dialog between what she calls "the beepers and the beeped." One doctor told Sen, "I never knew I could admit that I hate these sounds." Sen's goal: The sounds should be functional and safe but also gentle and respectful.

Sen learned that manufacturers of medical devices don't coordinate their soundscapes, and rather design the alerts louder and sharper than necessary for fear of being sued if someone misses an alarm. "They prioritize the safety and functionality of the devices, and they compete against each other, which is fine, but the manufacturers don't take into account how these sounds affect the emotions of the patients, and whether the alarm for the heart monitor creates a dissonance with the beeping of the IV drip." Sen quotes Florence Nightingale, who is often called the founder of modern nursing: "Unnecessary noise is the cruelest absence of care."

For her mission to create a more soothing hospital environment, Sen found like-minded researchers in Elif Ozcan who leads the Critical Alarms Lab at Delft University of Technology in the Netherlands, and Joseph Schlesinger, an anesthesiologist at Vanderbilt Medical Center who also happens to be an accomplished jazz pianist.

She also learned that everybody experiences sound differently. "One man was bothered by the nurses' chat in the hallway, while his wife loved it because it made her feel less alone. Some prefer utter stillness; others experience stillness as overwhelmingly oppressive. It's not just about the volume." So, for Kaiser Permanente, Sen transformed a space in Colorado into an interactive area where people could try different sounds at the push of a button and report how it affected them. There was a common denominator: Almost all people found sounds of nature soothing.

Especially for hospice patients, Sen creates soundscapes that the patient can tailor with simple hand gestures. Movement sensors translate a wave of a hand into the sounds of ocean waves or a short symphony. Her gentle compositions remind the listener of waterfalls or rain drops, chimes or a rainforest in the wind.

The pandemic has increased attention for her work because during the last year, millions have died and suffered in hospital beds without the soothing presence of their loved ones. Sen shares that some researchers believe that our sense of sound is the last sense to leave us when we die. Remembering her grandmother who died surrounded by beeping machines, Sen asked people from all over the world, "What is the last sound you want to hear at the end of your life?" Many wish for the sounds of nature, the laughter of children, or the voice of a loved one, and Sen recorded their wish lists for her project "My Last Sound".

What's the last sound she'd like to hear herself? Yoko Sen giggles, hesitates, but then she admits what she recorded: her husband's farting. "He's farting a lot, it is a familiar sound for me, and it makes me laugh. If that's the last sound I hear and I leave life laughing, that's a beautiful vision for me."

Pleasure-Centric Grief Care

Just as death care can be transformed by focusing on pleasure, so can grief care—both while you are caring for a dying loved one and after they have passed.

Today's model of grieving is sorrow-centric. This probably won't surprise you by now, but I believe that that model, too, should be pleasure-centric. It also probably won't surprise you by now that I sometimes encounter resistance by grieving loved ones who feel guilty about the prospect of thinking about pleasure as they grieve. "I shouldn't think about feeling good when something this sad is going on," I hear.

I understand this belief.

And so, gently, let us start by defining grief, which is where I start when I talk with grieving caretakers and survivors.

Grief is often defined as the pain or sorrow associated with loss. However, anyone who has really embraced their grieving will say it is also so much more than that. Currently, many practitioners describe grief as a range of emotions, behaviors, and physiological experiences that ebb and flow, undulate and meander. In other words, grief is a journey—a journey of huge emotions. And it can become a grand adventure if we are willing to honor those emotions by feeling them fully through our bodies. When we dare to feel fully, we feel *good*. Righteously so. For instance, a big old howling, screaming sobfest can feel exquisite at any point in the act, if it's embraced and cherished as the soul-nourishing act that it is.

Grieving becomes an elevated, sacred rite when we are willing to do this—willing to fully feel all of what wants to come through. We become aware of our majestic capacity for emotion, our infinite capacity to love. We are rendered more deeply human, more fully ourselves, more at home *within* ourselves. We have accessed the sheer space and permission to have all that is available to be felt and thus transform an experience of heavy stuckness into something life-affirming and possibly even transcendent.

"This feels wrong."

Even with a more generous definition of grief, however, many caretaking and surviving grievers express that it feels wrong to make a point of feeling good when a person they love is dying or has just died. They say they'd feel guilty going off to get a massage, eat at their favorite restaurant, or going for a walk when they could spend that time in the hospital or hospice room with their beloved. "It seems selfish to take that time away," they say. "And it seems selfish to actually let myself feel good when something so sad is happening."

What I tell them is that they are actually performing a service. By tending to their own pleasure, I say, they are putting good into the world in the form of one more person who is gratified enough to tend not only to their own well-being, but to that of others, even if simply in the form of being a worthy role-model.

I also encourage caretakers and surviving grievers to find what feels good to them in the moment to do according to their own standards. For instance, if it doesn't feel right to go get a massage, then perhaps go outside for a few minutes and use a handheld massage tool to work out the knots in your neck or back. The point is to take some time to tend to your own well-being, and to thus be more available and present to your dying loved one.

Finally, I tell grieving clients that dying people often express to me a desire to not be a burden on a loved one. Taking a break to refresh yourself allows you to be more accessible and a better companion to your dying loved one—and also relieves them of a sense of being burdensome.

Pleasure-Centric Grief Care

When creating a grieving process that is pleasure-centric, the first step is to carve out space for that process. Carving out space might mean setting some real boundaries with the people closest to you. For instance, you can let them know that you need the next 1–2 hours to yourself without interruption, perhaps even and especially if they hear you crying. Let them know that you need that time to tend to your grief.

In the first bloom of grief, as the period after the shock of the loss fades and the reality of the void settles upon you like a weighted blanket, what can feel good is to let yourself cry uninterrupted until you can't cry any more. When you're done crying or silent-screaming or staring numbly out the window, pause, and ask yourself, "What would feel good to my body or my soul to do next?"

And then, do whatever that is.

Don't Forget to Breathe

After that initial heavy phase, a good place to begin is to simply stop and breathe. No special technique required. Just notice the air coming in and going out of your body. This immediate connection to the body can allow information to flow up through you and inform the next activity. You can add a pleasurable element by asking yourself what would feel good to do now. It might be cleaning or fixing a broken object or dancing or eating something savory. No need to find the perfect thing, though. Just do what is easy and feels the best for as long as it feels good, and then do the next thing.

This, by the way, is the most reliable way to tap into the fact that you are alive: realizing each breath as a reminder that you're still here.

Pleasure-Centric Death Care Bullet Instructions

For easy reference, please find below a step-by-step roadmap of the pleasure-centric death care and grief care points I've explained above.

- Put your attention on the person who is dying. Consider what aspects of their past and current life brought delight to all their senses: taste, touch, sight, sound, smell, and thought.
- Gather the items necessary to ensure your loved one's pleasure, and plan for bigger events. For example, if you want to bring your loved one's church choir to perform in her room because she loves their music, make those arrangements.
- Ensure that their basic comfort needs are being met.
- Consider what might make getting those basic needs met feel even better for your beloved.
- Check in with him and make him an offer. (For example, if he enjoys jazz, perhaps offer to share a live performance by Miles Davis via YouTube.) Start with the minimum and gradually increase until it feels the best. If he is no longer able to speak, make your best educated guess.
- Continue to pay attention, check in, and discontinue any item or activity when it feels like enough.

Pleasure-Centric Grief Care Bullet Instructions

- Attend to your basic needs.
- Put your attention on yourself. Make an inventory of items and activities that make you feel good.
- Note which of those items/activities really "spark joy." Another way to look at this step is to consider what brings delight to all your senses: taste, touch, sight, sound, smell, and thought.
- Gather the items necessary and plan as is helpful to ensure your pleasure.

- Post a list or create a schedule.
- Refer to the list whenever you feel stuck or particularly down.

Death and Grieving Reimagined

We live in a culture that is so frightened of death, sorrow, and the "dark" that we separate these natural processes from the rest of life. It is normal to perceive them as abnormal, shameful, something to hide from, something to be shocked by—even though we will all die and also likely experience the grief of someone we love dying.

What if, though, we brought these processes into the light? What if we took the radical leap of letting them take us higher by insisting that they, too, are a part of the life cycle and that they, too, can—*must*—be pleasurable?

It is my hope that you will take this leap, or at least dip in a toe. Pleasure is a healing force that wants nothing from us, hurts no one, and makes everyone it touches feel good. It is my belief that we bring Heaven to Earth when we bring pleasure to our bodies as we live. And via my clients, it is my witnessed experience that pleasure allows us to live right up until the moment we die.

The use of poetry and movement can truly augment a grief journey. Naila Francis's experience is a testament to that.

Naila is a death midwife, offering practical, emotional, and spiritual guidance to navigate the threshold of death and to plan for its inevitability. She is also a certified From Grief to Gratitude™ coach, offering a safe and nurturing space to acknowledge and share grief.

❧ Let It All Hold You ❧

I am writing a poem about my dad's last trip to the hospital before he died. I have penned many poems about him, his death, and our relationship in the near-decade since I sat at his bedside in St. Lucia, where he took his final breath. Some have come like balm at the approach of an anniversary, a milestone we won't share. Some I've written to self-soothe or capture a memory, to reflect on the passages traversed in my grief.

But this poem is a struggle. I begin it during a grief writing workshop with a local poet I decide to take when I return home to Philadelphia, months after my dad's death. The inspiration for the assignment is Tim O'Brien's book, *The Things They Carried*, about what the men in his platoon toted while fighting in Vietnam. What was something my dad carried? Whether imagined or known, this is the invitation to write.

Even though I wasn't there, I choose to focus on the day my dad left for the hospital. To imagine what he packed in the small, brown suitcase I would see when I arrived, where his eyes lingered as he surveyed his home, the memories he visited…how somehow he knew this would be the last of his hospital stays.

I put the poem down, for months, years. Pick it up again. Let it go. Cry every time.

Some days, I let my body be the poem—a closing line I tack to another piece of writing that has nothing to do with my dad but a walk in winter. The fields fresh with snow, the lake frozen, life humming under the solitude, the silence, my ears cupped to the barest promise of spring. This, too, is a grief practice, for when the page is blank or the lines tangle, wait for the unfolding of something I need to know.

To step out into nature is to move my body with a rhythm that says, you, too, are of earth. It is to carry water. Know how to bend and flow. Sometimes I hum. Sometimes a song floats from the trees, the sky, bubbles up on my lips. I welcome any expression, make myself available to praise, to marvel…not instead of sorrow, but as companions. A way to drink in the world, stay open to more than the bleeding, the sting. To notice how my body makes room, is more spacious, always more spacious, than my grief would have me believe.

I learn of sorrow giving way to joy and joy to sorrow, how they are gatekeepers for each other. One night in Zumba, my body electric with the music, the happiness that fills me when I dance, I am stunned by tears. They seep out, even as I keep moving, a river that wants release. My wet eyes surprise me less in yoga, after the twists, the heart-openers, every wringing and expanding of what's constricted, stuck.

Eventually I will see a therapist and an energy healer. But for now, I dance, I walk, I come to my mat. And I keep writing poems.

Nine years later, I decide the hospital poem is finished. I call it "Leave-taking." Keep the ending.

"I don't think I'm going to make it, Julie." The line I imagine my dad said to his caregiver, and then one of my own: "Words he carried for weeks."

I still can't read this poem dry-eyed. It is sorrow moving through me—regret, absence, longing, wonder, my grief naked and sprawled in my chest. How does one carry his dying, live daily with what is vanishing? The questions thicken in my throat, pool in my eyes. And so does the love.

The poem holds it all.

Which is why I often turn to poetry in grief groups, with clients and in my own personal practice. The writing of poems. The reading of them. The listening and the noticing: where in the body do the words land? What do they touch, activate, console? What truths are called forth?

For the poem is a place of truth. When I share poetry with grievers, I'm interested in where language intersects with their lived experience, what the poem reveals, surfaces. The poem as validation, mirror, and even tender care. With writing, I encourage: tell the thing you're most afraid to say, the truth you haven't expressed. And if you don't know what that is, trust that moving a pen across the page is a dropping into the heart. A witnessing and a holding.

That to work the marrow of your grief—a pen in hand, a body in motion—is to ultimately make way for joy, pleasure, reverence…all that deepens your capacity to be fully alive in this world.

Epilogue

"Though we have all encountered our share of grief and troubles, we can still hold the line of beauty, form, and beat—no small accomplishment in a world as challenging as this one. Hard times require furious dancing. Each of us is the proof."
— Alice Walker, *Hard Times Require Furious Dancing: New Poems*

By now you know why it's hard to pursue a life of pleasure, especially as it relates to death, dying, and grief. As we wind down our journey together, I want to conclude with some thoughts on why I feel we must pursue pleasure at precisely the most challenging moments in our lives.

Often, when faced with seemingly insurmountable obstacles, I've been known to proclaim, "Must be time to party!" Ms. Walker and I—indeed, many of us glorious folk out here on the margins of "imperialist white-supremacist capitalist patriarchy" (in gratitude to Bell Hooks for this exquisitely succinctly accurate assessment of the culture)—have known the power of this sentiment. Not only is it cultural, it is also epigenetic. When Walker declares, "Each of us is proof," I posit that she is, in fact, referring to this essential aspect of resilience that has been passed down to us via our very DNA.

The need for pleasure and joy is an inherent quality of being human. Yet out here in the borderlands where "other" is allowed to exist, this quality becomes life-sustaining. In these borderlands, where life is a bit more tenuous and, thusly, its celebration necessarily more potent, there must be drops of joy, like water, to keep us going. We must feel good to keep going.

In the liminal space of the borderlands, out here beyond the rigid rules of normalcy, we also find the bookends of life. Still, the territory is quickly being ceded to the medical industrial complex. Yet for some inexplicable (at least to Them) reason, that territory is being resolutely reclaimed by some of us folks from the margins. So let us make use of the spaciousness that is available out here at the far reaches of life itself, this place of mystery—aka, death, dying, grief—where most fear to tread.

In this powerful and spacious portal within which life comes and goes, why not use the wisdom that is there waiting to be accessed in our own bodies, minds, and hearts? For out beyond rigid Eurocentric social mores is a knowing that beauty, form, and a good beat can ease the way because it remains life-sustaining; a remembrance that dying is still living; a sense that death is just life-force energy transmuted to non-physical form. And because, out here in the borderlands, we know there is so much more to life than the physical.

Nothing more is required in these seminal moments than to be still and know. Know that you are energy inhabiting a physicality composed of a variety of matter literally stretching across space and time, energy (spirit, consciousness) that wants to grow and transform in the best of ways—ways that include gain & loss, joy & love, living & dying.

Be still and know that you are eternal, that you are God.

For when you do, you will know, too, that pleasure is your birthright and indeed your saving grace.

And that knowing is worthy of furious dancing.

Made in the USA
Las Vegas, NV
07 December 2022